Should <u>You</u> Quit Before You're Fired?

by Paul Zane Pilzer

The writings of Professor Pilzer and Mr. Yarnell are
independent of each other and any product or service.

Second Printing / June 1993

0 9 8 7 6 5 4 3 2

ISBN 1-883599-00-8

Published by **Quantum Leap**
2700 Old Ranch Road
Carson City, Nevada 89704

Printed in the United States of America

Typesetting by Todd C. South
Cover design by Sandy Schmidt

What People Have Been Saying About
Unlimited Wealth and **Paul Zane Pilzer's**
Six-Point Theory of Economic Alchemy

`NATIONAL PRESS`

"His theory is crystal clear and applicable to anyone ... *Unlimited Wealth* is bound to revolutionize the way we view the nation's economy, if not our own lives. Pilzer challenges us to scrap not only the way we think about our daily affairs but the way we prepare ourselves for the future."

Newark Star-Ledger, February 18, 1991

"...explains how today's billionaires will create their wealth by producing goods and services that did not exist at the time of their birth ... a good theory that has implicitly become part of modern economic thinking."

National Review, March 18, 1991

"...the antidote to Ravi Batra." (author of *The Great Depression of 1990*)

The Dallas Morning News, February 17, 1991

"This book is as refreshing as a tulip in April. Paul Zane Pilzer has compiled some of the intellectual building blocks that hold expansion theories together ... things often lost in the daily exchange of news and information."

Detroit Free Press, February 10, 1991

"There is much to like in *Unlimited Wealth*. Pilzer's arguments are refreshingly unrooted in any single ideological camp."

Washington Monthly, February 1991

"...explains why even in the midst of a Persian Gulf war we have a glut of oil and the lowest prices in decades."

Chicago Sun-Times, February 10, 1991

"His solutions on competing with Japan, the environment, education, drugs and affordable housing are worth reading about. *Unlimited Wealth* will have a long shelf life."

The (Cleveland) Plain Dealer, February 10, 1991

"In the alchemic world in which we now live, a society's wealth is still a function of its physical resources, as traditional economics has long maintained. But unlike the outdated traditional economist, the alchemist of today recognizes that technology controls both the definition and the supply of physical resources."

National Journal, March 16, 1991

LEADING BUSINESS PEOPLE

"I'm amazed at your business capacity and, as well, your ability to put into laymen's terms the alchemic process. I know it will be well-received and a huge success."

Sam Walton, Chairman, Wal-Mart Stores

"It was with intense interest that I read and re-read **Unlimited Wealth** ... you can be assured that it will make a significant contribution to our society."

Dr. Stanley Pearle, Founder, Pearle Vision Centers

"Pilzer and **Unlimited Wealth** can give you the equivalent of a college education in just a few hours. He explains not only where the greatest economic opportunities lie today, but what you can do to take advantage of them."

Dexter Yager, President, Yager International

BOOK REVIEW PUBLICATIONS

"Alchemy, a dynamic new view ad odds with classical economics, best describes our advanced economy now. The Alchemic world isn't just a promising model, a hypothetical theory or an abstract dream. It is in fact, the world in which we live."

Soundview Executive Book Summaries, March 1991

"...a paradigm-buster. His application of alchemic principles to public education, child care and immigration is brilliant. If somehow every person in the United States Congress could absorb the content of this book, public policy would greatly benefit. And Pilzer's two chapters on Japan, especially his discussion of 'Why Japan Isn't Going To Make It,' is a modern-day classic."

Nexus Commentary, May 20, 1991

"This work is so revolutionary that we can only recommend that you read it from cover to cover and in the order presented. We also suggest that you set aside time to read it more than once, and that you prepare to highlight and make notes. We predict that you will immediately want to share **Wealth's** ideas with colleagues and associates."

Business Book Review, Summer 1991

BEST-SELLING AUTHORS

"I must confess that, judging the title, I at first thought you were a crackpot. However, having read the first line I understood how wrong I was. From that moment I could not put it down."

*Dr. Martin van Creveld, author of **Technology and War***

"...your fundamental thesis is so brilliantly simple that it is beyond refutation."

*Robert Elegant, author of **Pacific Destiny***

"...your theory of economic alchemy is brilliant because it explains to everyday people what is happening around them and, more importantly, how they can use this knowledge to shape their future."

Anthony Robbins, author of ***Awaken the Giant Within***
and ***Unlimited Power.***

Table of Contents

traditional business for suggesting that individuals should and can take control of their own destinies while Professor Pilzer's view is at odds with classic economics because of his similar belief system.

In this brief series of essays you will find the answers to some very critical questions about your future. You will gain very important insights which range from what to suggest that your kids study in school to how and why the corporate life of the past is rapidly becoming obsolete. You will see yourself in these pages because to read Professor Pilzer's work is to gaze into a mirror in which you will come face to face with your present and future reality as opposed to the theoretical and hypothetical abstractions found in other such books.

When you are finished *you will know exactly how America got into our present economic situation*, where we're headed, and how to best capitalize on this information. Of critical importance to most people is whether the field of Network Marketing, given current economic trends, is really for them and we'll attempt to specifically answer that question.

The reason you were given this book is because someone believes you have the inherent potential to escape the rat race of traditional business and build a large, dynamic Network Marketing organization. That person invested in you because he or she believes that you have what it takes to succeed. What they also believe is that a person like you will not change careers unless a very credible analysis leads you to conclude that such a decision would be both prudent and in your family's best interest. Few people have the credibility that Professor Pilzer has in the field of economics, and only a handful have built a 30,000 person downline in the field of Network Marketing as I was blessed to do in my first three years. I hope that Professor Pilzer's economic insights are revealing to you and that my periodic commentaries shed some light on why Network Marketing is such a viable industry, particularly at this time.

The manner in which we collaborated was quite simple. Professor Pilzer sent me, in essay form, several of the chapters he had completed for one of his next books and in strategic places I added commentary, which you will find in quotes, designed to specifically elucidate how his points apply directly to our industry. It is, to our knowledge, the first time two individual authors with divergent backgrounds have worked in a concerted effort to truly assess current and future economic trends which affect us all.

Professor Pilzer is not involved in Network Marketing and I'm certainly no economist. But we both recognize that many people who read this book are in the process of making decisions which will dramatically impact their families . Many of you will unfortunately be fired from traditional businesses during the next decade and others of you have come to recognize that it's not for you in the first place. Franchises are an option to your current plight, but you better be prepared to invest anywhere from $100,000 to $1 million and understand that last year 33% of all franchises lost money, 33% broke even and 33% made a profit.

As an acquaintance of mine who recently sold his McDonald's franchise in order to become involved in the Network Marketing company Nu Skin stated, "I invested a million dollars and a free and clear corner lot, and for several years I was just a shift change supervisor for a bunch of pimply-faced kids before I ever broke even."

Going back to school is an option, but over 75% of all graduates in the past 10 years failed to get jobs in the fields in which they majored. Starting your own "ma and pa" operation is an option, but 90% of those upstart companies are bankrupt in the first five years. And remaining in corporate America is an option as is changing companies every 4 or 5 years, but you better be prepared to give up all of your time and feel constantly overworked in what *Time* magazine calls "the rat race that is killing us."

Until corporate America cleans up its act, assuming it ever does, Network Marketing is your most viable option. It generally requires under $300 to get started. Never become involved with a front-end-load company which requires thousands of dollars in product investments. You can begin part time, need no office, employees or overhead, and can earn over $100,000 your very first year with hard work. Get back with the person who gave you this book and take a serious look at their business opportunity because there is one thing we are absolutely certain about: distribution is your key to financial prosperity over the next 20 years and Network Marketing is the ultimate new mode of distribution. And by the way, each concept explained in this book applies to doctors, lawyers, accountants, teachers and other professionals. Especially affected are those already unemployed as well as those who own franchises or small businesses.

Drop your preconceived biases about pyramids and realize that the pyramid is found on the back of our U.S. dollar bills because it is the most successful and enduring structure our founding fathers ever envisioned for free enterprise. What makes the Network Marketing pyramid more effective than the government, educational or corporate pyramids is that instead of one person at the very top becoming wealthy, we each have the opportunity to rise to our full potential. From tenured professors at the very top of our college pyramids, men and women who can't lose their jobs, to Fortune 500 presidents of major airlines who earn 1,700 times more than entry level flight attendants, the traditional pyramid has become economically unfair. In Network Marketing everyone begins at the top of their own pyramid and can rise to dramatic income levels through personal performance not arbitrary raises which aren't tied to productivity. Network Marketing could be your shot at absolute wealth and time freedom. . .don't miss it by remaining closed minded.

Above all else, don't disrupt the ethical aspects of our industry by seeking out any person other than the one who gave you this book. Because that person thought enough of you to introduce you to this marvelous industry, they earned the right to profit from your efforts should you ultimately choose to become involved with their company. Very early in your exposure to this industry, before you understand the unwritten code of ethics, a few unethical distributors might attempt to take advantage of your innocence by recommending that you bypass the person who gave you this book and sign up under them instead. That's a direct violation of our industry's code of ethics. The honest way is to sign up directly under the person who introduced you to the company and then never switch to another person's downline for any reason. Some unethical distributors might try to persuade you that you will do better under them because of their experience, ties to the home office, or dramatic income levels. Nothing could be further from the truth. Your success in Network Marketing will be directly tied to your own efforts. Of course it's important that you select a solvent company with consumable products and that your upline leaders have a history of supporting their people. Remember, if your immediate sponsor is not able to meet your needs, all you need to do is track upline until you find someone successful who has a vested interest in your success.

Finally, realize that Network Marketing, while potentially more lucrative than any other profession, involves hard work, dedication and two to three years of commitment to one company. Those who suggest to you that this is a get-rich-quick scheme or that you don't have to retail products are simply lying or ignorant. Good luck in your search for Camelot. I found mine in Network Marketing and my fervent prayer is that you will do the same. By the way, what are your other options?

Mark Yarnell
Lake Tahoe
November 1992

Introduction

"Daddy, daddy," exclaimed the boy running from the front porch carrying a ball and baseball bat. Watch this!"

Upon approaching the father the boy tossed the ball into the air and swung the bat, completely missing the ball by over a foot.

"Strike one," shouted the son. "Now watch this one." The boy tossed the ball into the air again, this time swinging so hard that he almost lost his balance as he completely missed the ball.

"Strike two," shouted the son, even louder. "Now, for the final pitch." The boy choked up on the bat, planted his heels firmly on the driveway, and threw the ball high into the air. As the ball returned to earth he swung so hard that he completely spun around and collapsed on the hard pavement, again missing the ball by over a foot.

"Strike three," shouted the boy panting on the ground from his fall.

The father put down his briefcase and helped the exhausted boy get up from the driveway, trying to hide the disappointment he felt at his son's failure.

"So, what do you think," exclaimed his son. "Not bad for a pitcher, huh Dad."

❋ ❋ ❋

This story, which was told to me by a cherished friend, Leon Rabin, illustrates part of what this book is about.

We live in a time of unprecedented world peace, and, for those of us fortunate enough to live in countries like the United States, Western Europe, or Japan, a time of unprecedented prosperity. As we approach the twenty-first century we can truly say that we live in the age dreamed about by the ancient alchemists who sought peace and prosperity by trying to discover how to turn ordinary metals into gold.

For today, advancing technology has given us the ability to make much more than the mere gold dreamed about by our ancestors. We raise our fish in desert fish farms, we have conquered most of our major diseases, and we have at hand, for all practical purposes, an unlimited supply of the natural resources we once fought wars over. Perhaps most telling, our greatest wealth is derived from our ability to electronically collect and process information with silicon chips *which we derive from sand.*

In the twentieth century in which we live, humankind's economic output has already exceeded the previous one hundred centuries of recorded history. And yet, as we approach the final years of our greatest century, fewer and fewer of us *feel* rich.

> **"One of the reasons fewer of us feel wealthy in spite of our unprecedented economic prosperity is because we don't have the time freedom to enjoy our money. Network Marketing affords the average individual both the opportunity for dramatic wealth as well as the most sought after and precious commodity in America: Free time."**
> **—Mark B. Yarnell**

For some of us personally, or for someone we know and love, it seems as if the alchemic age has passed us by. And for most of us, even though we intellectually *know* how much better off we are than our forebears, sometimes it seems as if we're trapped in the Red Queen's race—having to run faster and faster merely to stay in the same place.

But perhaps most distressing of all, even for those of us who do feel successful, few among us seem to understand *why*— why some of us are succeeding, why some of us are failing, and why some of us are standing still.

It seemed so simple in the past. The recipe for success was to go to school, choose an occupation or a company, and work in that field or for that company for the rest of your life. Looking back on just the past ten years, the only thing clear is that this former recipe for success is now a recipe for disaster!

> *"The recipe for success in Network Marketing is enthusiasm, duplication and hard work. We have been programmed into believing that the 40 year plan is the key to success and security. But today's generation of Baby Boomers aren't buying into this old-school philosophy. Educational background, age, sex, color and experience are of no real value to the person who enters this field. Network Marketing is called the 'great equalizer' because everyone has an equal chance."*
>
> **—Mark B. Yarnell**

In 1985 there were approximately 100,000 people employed in a $24 billion industry manufacturing vinyl records— virtually all of whom were displaced as the digital CD swept the music business by 1990. Who could have foreseen in 1985 that an almost 100 year old industry which survived, even thrived, through two world wars, would dissolve itself in less than five percent of the 100 years it took to develop?

In 1979 approximately 300,000 people were employed designing, manufacturing, and repairing mechanical carburetors—almost all of whom were similarly displaced by the electronic fuel injector in 1985.

These and thousands of other similar technological changes caused the displacement of 20 million blue collar workers in the 1980s as it became socially acceptable in the U.S. to fire, rather than keep and retrain, workers in obsolete occupations.

Those Americans who chose the other recipe for success, avowing loyalty to a company rather than to a specific occupation, have fared even worse. Thousands of companies have found that in a rapidly changing world they can no longer afford to honor their unwritten contract to take care of the employees who used to take care of them.

> *"Today's Baby Boomers are fed up with broken promises and unfulfilled contracts. They are looking at non-traditional entrepreneurial ventures to fill the gaps left by corporate 'fat-trimming,' hostile take-overs and mergers."*
> **—Mark B. Yarnell**

The upright management teams that did try to honor this unwritten contract of post-war America have already found either their companies out of business or their positions sold out by stockholders to new management teams—teams sometimes so young that they are often unaware that such an unwritten contract might even have existed.

And yet, despite the ever present complaints in the media and the demagoguery from our politicians, as we shall see throughout this book, the cold hard fact is that we are richer than ever before. Far richer. But why, you may ask, is this fact that we are far richer *cold and hard*?

The fact that we are far richer than ever before is cold and hard because unlike previous periods of economic prosperity, our current wave of prosperity is not a wave at all, sweeping along in its wake all with whom it comes in contact. Our current wave of prosperity only looks like a wave when measured in total terms like gross national product or total retail sales.

In reality, our current wave of prosperity is more like a jagged mountain range—large and strong but with ever increasing peaks and troughs. And like a large jagged mountain range, although the entire range may be significantly above sea level, your perception of how high or low it is depends almost entirely on the internal vantage point from which you view it.

For the record companies headquartered in Los Angeles, the switch to digital CDs was a godsend as they now sell twice the dollar volume of digital CDs that they used to sell of vinyl records. But to the vinyl record manufacturing plants in Ohio and Pennsylvania, the so-called Recession of 1991 came as early as 1985 and still shows no sign of retreating.

> *"When I entered the field of Network Marketing, I had no business or technical skills of any kind. Yet by my fourth full month I was earning over $15,000 a month through hard work alone. More exciting is the fact that I'll never be plagued by any technological changes nor can anyone displace me or terminate me for any reason. That's the real security of Network Marketing."*
> **—Mark B. Yarnell**

For the high technology manufacturers of electronic fuel injectors, and for society at large, the switch from mechanical carburetors created a whole new industry with tremendous social benefits—less reliance on foreign oil, a halving of automobile air pollution, and less frequent automobile breakdowns. But to the former carburetor mechanics and manufacturers who didn't have the skills (or the will) to switch to electronic fuel injection, America is just not the same kind of place anymore. However, when we closely examine the signs around us of supposed economic decline—unemployment, loss of manufacturing jobs, an increasing trade deficit, bank failures—like our aspiring little league pitcher, we see our reality in a different light. Many, if not most, of these supposed signs of economic decline are actually a displacement from one sector of our economy to another.

More importantly, most of these supposed signs of decline actually represent a significant net increase in our total economic wealth. In fact, as we shall see throughout this book, barring unforeseen changes in our tax structure or national economic policy, due to the types of economic changes we are experiencing, our total economic wealth literally has no place to go but up.

> *"The real question to ask yourself is this: 'As our economic prosperity continues to go no place but up, will you dedicate yourself to making a handful of people at the top of some corporate pyramid wealthy? Or will you enter Network Marketing giving yourself control of your own destiny ... the same control you learned as a child and lost as an adult?'"*
> **—Mark B. Yarnell**

In 1930 the U.S. needed approximately 30 million farmers to support the agricultural requirements of 100 million Americans. During the next 50 years, advances in chemical and biological science made farms and food production so efficient that by 1980 only 300,000 farmers were needed, producing more than 150 percent of the agricultural requirements of almost 300 million Americans.

While this represented a 100-fold decrease in agricultural employment and a 300-fold increase in production efficiency per farmer, this great change in the American employment landscape took place over 50 years or so, roughly two generations. This was enough time for most of our farmers to peacefully retire and for their children to become vinyl record manufacturers or carburetor mechanics.

Unfortunately, the children or grandchildren of these farmers weren't so lucky as changes that occurred over 50 years in their parents lives occurred over five or ten years in theirs.

This simple truth about the accelerating pace of technological change lies at the core of our economic situation today. Changes in society that used to occur over 50 years now occur in five or ten. And if an examination of the past decade reveals anything, it is that the increase in the pace of technological advancement in the 1980s was only the beginning.

In the past, when few of these types of changes took place over a single lifetime, they were of little more than passing interest to anyone other than a few academic economists and historians. Although we traditionally define our forebears very existence by the technology of the age in which they lived—the Stone Age, the Iron Age, the Industrial Age, etc.— people were born and died within one of these ages so technological changes did not affect their daily existence.

Now, when technological changes take place rapidly over a single career, they are the single largest factor in deciding success or failure. The overwhelmingly largest determinant of success today for both the individual and the organization is the speed with which they can accept, learn, and work with technological change. The old adage of achieving success by learning something well through diligence and perseverance doesn't go very far when the task is often obsolete by the time it is mastered. Prosperity today belongs to the person and organization that learns new things the fastest.

> *"Those who recognize the changes occurring in distribution through the low-risk, minimal investment field of Network Marketing will undoubtedly become the billionaires of tomorrow. As today's billionaire founders of Wal-Mart, Amway and Federal Express have proven, distribution is the wave of the future. The industrial, agricultural and information ages have come and gone leaving distribution as the only remaining, stable era. Those who choose to participate will undoubtedly prosper."*
> **—Mark B. Yarnell**

And finally, that is what this book is all about. Changes. Changes that used to take place in our society over generations now take place in decades. And the people who will benefit the most are the ones who understand why and how this is happening.

CHAPTER I
The Search For Camelot

The great Christian theologian St. Augustine (354-430 A.D.) was once asked what God did before He created the universe. Augustine's reply: He was busy preparing Hell for the people who would ask such questions.

Today, most of us do ask—and encourage our children to ask—such questions. For today, even though we do not have all the answers, we are surer than ever before that there are answers—and that it is our God-given destiny as human beings to discover them.

And yet, in the one area where most of us spend the majority of our waking hours—economics, earning our livelihoods—few of us feel that we have found the answers we seek.

Some of us have seen our economic aspirations frustrated. And most of us, even though we intellectually know how much better off we are each year on a material basis, feel trapped, having to run faster and faster merely to stay in the same place.

Perhaps most distressing of all, those among us who seem to have found the answers—by achieving financial success—seem incapable of teaching what we've learned to help others, sometimes even to members of our own families.

"Teaching others exactly how we did succeed is the very basis of Network Marketing. The key for new distributors is finding a mentor in their upline organization who is successful and duplicating exactly what that person has done. New distributors should never try to re-invent the wheel."

—**Mark B. Yarnell**

The 1967 movie *The Graduate* offered with confidence a one word answer to economics for an aspiring college graduate—"plastics." How many of us could answer our children with similar confidence if they graduated from high school or college today and asked the same question.

It seemed so simple in the past. The recipe for success was to go to school, choose an occupation or a company, and work hard in that field or for that company for the rest of your life. Looking back on just the past ten years, the only thing clear today is that this former recipe for success has become a recipe for disaster!

"In Network Marketing, educational background and former business experience are of little value. The real recipe for success consists in finding a debt free, solvent company with consumable, commonly-used products and then working diligently for 24-36 months. The extent of one's success is generally in direct relation to one's enthusiasm, self-confidence and positive attitude — all of which are natural by-products of this business."

— **Mark B. Yarnell**

Whether in helping us plan our future as individuals, or in finding ways to take care of the increasing numbers of poor in our society, virtually the only thing that our so-called experts—our economists—can agree on, is that they can no longer agree on almost anything. Economists have begun qualifying their predictions and prescriptions with phrases such as "on the other hand...," a state of affairs that once led President Truman to remark that what the United States needed was a good one-handed economist.

The science of economics today has advanced only to where the science of medicine was at the beginning of the 19th century. Before we discovered the underlying theories that explained bacterial infections, and thus inoculations and antibiotics, we knew from experience what few medicines and treatments worked—applications. However, without an underlying theory explaining why, we were unable to learn and grow from our experiences. Moreover, only a select few could afford what little medical care existed.

Once we developed working theories underlying our medical observations, good medical care became widespread. In just a few decades we conquered almost all of the diseases—smallpox, typhoid, polio—that had been the scourge of mankind for millenniums.

When it comes to searching for a working economic theory that we can apply to both our lives as individuals and to the problems of our society, there is much to be learned from studying medical history. The people who created the great medical breakthroughs—men and women like Louis Pasteur, Marie Curie, Jonas Salk, and Paul Ehrlich—never doubted for a moment that there was a solution, that human beings were not put on Earth to suffer. They believed that their faith in the higher being of their choice would lead them out of the darkness.

> *"We've seen evidence many times that one of the primary personality traits of the successful Network Marketer is altruism and belief in a higher power. Creating a goal bigger than one's self is a major factor in achieving wealth and time freedom, especially in this industry. The high point in my networking career was when I was able to donate $150,000 to the Reno United Way in 1991."*
> **— Mark B. Yarnell**

In contrast, most of the original founders of the science we now call economics, and many practitioners of the science today, do not hold such lofty ideals as the ultimate outcome of their work. Many economists today believe that the world in which we live is one of scarce resources—and the best that they can hope for is to discover a better or more fair way of distributing what we have amongst ourselves. No wonder they call economics "the dismal science!"

This "economic" view of the world directly contrasts with the teachings of all of our great religions. Virtually no religious person today could accept that a true and just God would have created a world where one person's gain would have to be another person's loss.

> *"In Network Marketing, one need never jeopardize his reputation in order to succeed because this is a win-win business in which we all strive to elevate others. Dishonesty and unethical behavior are not profitable in Network Marketing, making our industry unique in all of free enterprise. In our business one person's gain is never another person's loss."*
> **— Mark B. Yarnell**

It is in this light that we begin our quest — a quest for a working theory of economics that is consonant with our belief that God, our Father, did not put us on Earth to profit at the expense of each other. Incorporated within this belief is our understanding that like a loving father, God would not simply hand over to us, His children, everything that we required. Rather, He would give us the tools that we needed and allow us to discover how to use them for ourselves.

> *"One of the reasons many people fail in Network Marketing is because they fall victim to the management trap. It's good to remember that God made the birds and the worms but He didn't go around dropping those worms in the nests. Leading by example, finding new people to bring into your organization, is the key to this industry."*
>
> **— Mark B. Yarnell**

CHAPTER II

Why Do We Have So Much Bad News?

We live today in a mass media environment where the companies who deliver us our news—television stations, newspapers, radio stations, magazines, etc.—are commercially dependent on maintaining our interest. And today, maintaining our interest means giving us a continual barrage of bad news.

In an increasingly complex world, fewer and fewer journalists understand the dramatic changes our economy undergoes each day, let alone the statistics—unemployment, gross national product, trade deficits—that accompany these changes. But most news directors and aspiring anchor persons know that bad news for the economy means good news for their nightly ratings and for their personal careers.

> *"Network Marketing distributors must be taught to expect controversial press as soon as their companies grow large enough to attract regulatory and media attention. The very survival of their companies will ultimately depend on the willingness of each distributor to remain loyal to his or her Network Marketing company while undergoing the inevitable scrutiny of the press."*
> — **Mark B. Yarnell**

The material lifestyle of almost every American has steadily risen since the end of the Second World War. Yet little of this is evident in our mass media which, when preparing the nightly news with tomorrow's headlines, must continually weigh maintaining our interest against a balanced reporting of the day's economic events.

For example, since 1960, every time the federal government releases statistics on the median price of a new house, we are treated to a barrage of how the average American can no longer afford a detached single-family home. Meanwhile, the media conveniently neglects to mention that the median size home Americans can supposedly no longer afford is more than twice the size of the median size home they supposedly could afford back in 1960, let alone the fact that it includes air conditioning, dishwashers, and countless other features that make it perhaps four times more valuable to its new occupant.[1]

In reality, the average cost of a new home, when just adjusted for consumer purchasing power and physical size— let alone technological improvements—has steadily fallen during the past 30 years. This is well evidenced by the fact that during the 1960-1990 period, the number of owner-occupied housing units increased from 33 million to 59 million homes, well in excess of the growth in the general population.[2]

More recently, in the early 1990s, when the price of existing homes—which had risen far above their replacement values in the inflationary 1980s—began coming down to more realistic and affordable levels, the media sensationalized this price adjustment as the sure sign of a coming depression. They failed to point out that the sale of a home at a lower-than-expected price is merely a transfer of wealth from a homeowner to a home buyer—every unhappy home seller made for a very happy home buyer.

The unprecedented rise in home prices during the 1980s represented a transfer of wealth from our younger citizens (homebuyers) to our older citizens (homeowners), and recent housing price adjustments merely reflect a return of some of these "unearned" gains to the next generation.

But this misreporting of the economic effect of home price declines is almost insignificant when it comes to the misunderstanding by the media of important economic issues like unemployment, trade deficits, and Gross National Product (GNP).

On unemployment, we regularly see heartbreaking reports of people unemployed due to the closing of local plants, without any follow-up reporting on what happens to these unfortunate individuals—which would show that one-third find new jobs at a 20 percent or more increase in salary.[3]

On trade deficits, we regularly hear that Japanese cars account for 3.7 million of the approximately 10 million vehicles sold in the United States—without hearing that over 2.2 million, or 61%, of these "Japanese" vehicles are manufactured in the U.S. (employing over 15 percent of all U.S. autoworkers).[4]

And on our Gross National Product, we regularly hear meaningless statistics quoted about the rise or fall in GNP without any relationship to what really matters—the purchasing power of the American consumer.

> *"In the late '50s and early '60s as franchises were finding their place in the American economy, they came within 11 votes of being banned by Congress because they were thought to be a pyramid scheme. And yet today, franchises make up one third of our GNP. It is predicted that Networking Marketing as a means of distribution will have an even greater impact on the purchasing power of the American consumer."*
> **— Mark B. Yarnell**

For example, when General Motors manufactures a 1993 $10,000 automobile with all the features of a $15,000 1988 model, the consumer enjoys a $5,000 increase in lifestyle while the media reports a $5,000 drop in GNP. Equally important, one of the largest components in the GNP is based on the value of all the homes in America—thus when home prices fall, it is negatively reported as a dramatic drop in GNP when, as long as there remains a buyer for the home at *some* price, it is merely a transfer in wealth from homeowners to home buyers.

Our mass media, due to their own misunderstanding of what's really going on in our economy, fail to report the economic information that matters most to ordinary Americans—what is really happening to their jobs, to the economic future of their country and most importantly to their lifestyles. However, at least for the major television networks, this lack of understanding certainly doesn't hinder them from grossly over-reporting bad news.

A university study of how television covers economic affairs—during periods when the GNP was both rising and falling—found that when GNP was rising, the number of stories devoted to the economy dropped 26%. More significantly, the number of stories reporting the quarterly-released key economic indicators dropped 64%—for every 10 stories reporting an announced numerical decrease in GNP, there were only 3.4 stories reporting a later corresponding increase.

As the sponsor of the study observed, newscasters can't seem to find a GNP figure that they like. "If the number is strong, they warn of an overheated economy and inflation; if it's weak, they worry about recession."[5]

---

1   The median size of a new home in the U.S. was approximately 1,000 square feet in 1960 and rose linearly to approximately 2,000 square feet in 1990.

2   The general U.S. population increased from approximately 180 million to 280 million persons (55% increase) during this period while the number of owner-occupied housing units increased from 33 million to 59 million (81% increase). U.S. Department of Commerce, Bureau of the Census, *Statistical Abstract of the United States: 1989* (Washington: Government Printing Office, 1991), 706.

3   A labor department study of 5.1 million workers displaced between 1979 and 1984 showed that nearly one-third had earnings gains of 20 percent or more, although one-fifth had taken pay cuts of 20 percent or more. Robert J. Samuelson, 'The American Job Machine," *Newsweek*, 23 February 1987, 57.

4   Pilzer, Paul Zane. *Unlimited Wealth—The Theory and Practice of Economic Alchemy* (Crown Publishers, 1991). pp. 179-181

5   Bodnar, Janet, "How TV Sees the Economy," *Changing Times*, December 1989, 89.

CHAPTER III
Unemployment—
The Greatest Challenge in the 1990s

"In the 1990s anyone who enters Network Marketing will have the largest number of potential distributors in history from which to recruit because of the existence of the largest pool of unemployed and displaced workers this country has seen since the Great Depression."
—**Mark B. Yarnell**

Ironically, unemployment is often the first sign of economic growth. When a worker's job is displaced by a machine or technological advance, the society as a whole is just as rich because it still receives the output of the displaced worker's labor (now performed by the machine). Moreover, our society becomes much richer when the temporarily-displaced individual finds a new job and we receive the benefits of both his or her old and new jobs.

Assume you own a restaurant that employs three people washing dishes at $10,000 each in annual wages or about $200 per week. Along comes a company that leases you an automatic dishwasher for $1000 a year, causing you to lay off the three employees washing dishes and saving you $30,000 a year. To the outside world, your business must be terrible— you just laid off three employees. But to your family, business is great. Your dishes are still being cleaned and you have available $29,000 per annum more to spend on additional goods and services. Or you can lower your prices by up to $29,000 per year and increase your volume and total profits still further.

Wall Street may not understand how unemployment in our economy is often the first sign of economic growth, but they surely understand the effect on individual companies. Throughout the so-called Recession of 1991, the Dow Jones average continually broke new records as it rose to over 3400 points, with many of the leading stocks being the companies doing the most layoffs.

And herein lies the major challenge for our society in the 1990s. The worker displaced by advancing technology never believes that he or she is going to find any job, let alone a new and better one. The reason is that we have an economic and educational system built on a model where a person is supposed to go to school, choose a profession or trade, and perform that function for the rest of their life.

> *"Going back and forth to the same job year after year after year may have met the needs of our parents' and grandparents' generation, but it doesn't satisfy the longing for fulfillment, challenge, security or quality of life by most people today. Network Marketing is one of the few mediums available to ordinary people that is both affordable and offers the potential of personal and time freedom."*
> **—Mark B. Yarnell**

Even where a displaced employee does have a specific skill that could be of value to a certain employer, or has the ability to rapidly advance by just being given an opportunity to learn something new, there does not exist today an efficient system for distributing and retraining these displaced employees to potential employers.

Moreover, technology moves so fast today that changes which used to occur in fifty years now occur in five or ten. While it took fifty years from 1930 to 1980 to go from needing 30 million to needing 300,000 farmers, it took only five years from 1980 to 1985 to go from 300,000 people in the carburetor business to less than 30,000—when computerized fuel injection became standard in every automobile. Or only five years from 1985 to 1990 to go from over 100,000 people manufacturing vinyl records to virtually none—when digital CD's took the record industry by storm.

Thus, while in the past we may not have needed an affirmative system for retraining technologically displaced employees and matching them up with prospective employers (because typically their children were retrained for different occupations as they retired), we critically need such a system today.

> *"Success in Network Marketing inevitably results when a person becomes skilled at recruiting, training and coaching displaced or unhappy workers. That is the essence of this business."*
> **—Mark B. Yarnell**

One of the greatest problems with retraining technologically displaced employees is that, almost by definition, many of the new jobs for them are just being created from society's demand for new products and new services—products and services that are purchased with the savings from the technological displacement (e.g., the $29,000 saved in the dishwasher example).

For example, in 1960 approximately 5 percent of the meals eaten by Americans were eaten outside the home in restaurants— going out to eat was only for special occasions or for very rich people. By 1980, owing to rising American affluence and an increasing variety of products offered by the food services industry, approximately 50 percent of the meals eaten by Americans were in restaurants. But, if someone were predicting back in 1960 that almost 20 percent of the U.S. employed population would find positions in the food service industry, who would have believed them? Not only was the demand not apparent for such a 1000 percent increase in the number of restaurant meals, but the restaurants themselves, as well as most of the shopping centers in which they would locate, didn't even exist in 1960.

Looking back, it is easy to see that the majority of our economy and our employment today is based on products and industries that didn't even exist when we were born. However, it is often difficult to similarly recognize that our greatest opportunities lie ahead—particularly at times of unemployment or personal economic crisis.

> *"Some of our greatest opportunities rise out of adversities. Network Marketing is one such example—it has always flourished in times of high unemployment and personal economic crisis."*
>
> **—Mark B. Yarnell**

CHAPTER IV
Distribution—
The Greatest Opportunity in the 1990s

In the 1967 movie *The Graduate*, the successful uncle summarized the key to wealth for his aspiring nephew in a single word: "plastics." Back then, the key to wealth for most people still lay in finding less expensive ways to make things.

Today, however, thanks to plastics and so many other better ways of making things, the key to wealth for most of us no longer lies in manufacturing existing products. For most people seeking wealth in the 1990s, the greatest opportunities lie in the distribution sector of our economy.

> *"When an economist with Nobel potential writes, 'for most people seeking wealth in the 1990s, the greatest opportunities lie in distribution' ...it might be wise for all of us to pay attention. Unless one has the capital to launch traditional stores like Wal-Mart, Network Marketing remains the best form of low overhead distribution in free enterprise. I converted $179 of borrowed capital into a distribution network which last year compensated me one and a half million dollars."*
> **—Mark B. Yarnell**

In the 1960s, a manufactured product that sold for $300, for example, a camera or a television set, typically had a manufacturing cost of approximately $150 and a distribution cost of approximately $150. Distribution costs back then accounted for approximately 50% of retail prices.

In the 1990s, the same product of similar quality typically retails for approximately $100 (although many people don't realize this because they have shifted to purchasing much higher quality products). This two-thirds price reduction for similar quality items has occurred primarily because innovative manufacturing methods have lowered the costs of production all the way from $150 to approximately $20 or less. Distribution costs have also fallen, from $150 to approximately $80, to where they now account for approximately 80 percent of the price for a typical $100 retail product.

TYPICAL RETAIL PRODUCT COST BREAKDOWN

	1960s		1990s	
Manufacturing Costs	$150	50%	$20	20%
Distributrion Costs	$150	50%	$80	80%
Total Retail Price	$300	100%	$100	100%

The reason that distribution costs have not fallen as much as manufacturing costs is that we have yet to apply to distributing things many of the innovative methods that we have already applied to making things.

"The most innovative new methods created in the field of distribution are ironically the very same principles upon which our nation of free enterprise was first established. They are the cornerstone principles of Network Marketing— word of mouth advertising, product excellence, and good old-fashioned hard work."
—Mark B. Yarnell

Thus, in the 1960s, it was possible to make a great deal of money by lowering the cost of producing things. Back then, even a 10 or 20 percent reduction in manufacturing costs could lower your retail price by $15 or $30. And great fortunes were made by those who found ways to lower manufacturing costs all the way from $150 to $20 or less, often by moving production facilities overseas.

In the 1990s, however, where manufacturing costs now represent less than $20 of a typical $100 retail price, a 10 or 20 percent reduction in manufacturing costs might only represent a $2 to $4 retail price reduction on a $100 item.

But in the 1990s, where distribution costs now represent more than $80 of a typical $100 retail price, a 10 or 20 percent reduction in distribution costs might represent an $8 to $16 retail price reduction on a $100 item. And a 50 percent or greater reduction in distribution costs—sometimes feasible by just eliminating one leg in the distribution chain between the factory and the consumer—might represent a $40 or even greater retail price reduction on a $100 item.

> *"A good Network Marketing company removes virtually every middleman between the producer and consumers, thus enabling its distributors to prosper and the company to enjoy long-term stability."*
> **—Mark B. Yarnell**

Due primarily to the increased role of distribution costs in our economy, most of the production facilities that moved overseas in the 1960s are now moving back to the U.S. In 1991 approximately 2.2 million of the 3.7 million Japanese cars sold in America were made in America. By 1994 it is expected that virtually all of the large television sets sold in America will be made in North America.

But more importantly, in the past two decades the majority of the greatest personal fortunes have been made by people who found better ways of distributing things rather than better ways of making things.

"Two of the wealthiest self-made billionaires in America made their fortunes in Network Marketing. In one such company, the average monthly income of their top 70 distributors in just their seventh year of business exceeded $70,000 ...that's right, $70,000 A MONTH!"
—**Mark B. Yarnell**

For example, in 1992 the richest man in America was a person who had only started his company in the 1960s and never made anything in his life—the late Sam Walton who founded Wal-Mart. Or the person who became a billionaire by founding an entire airline in the 1970s for moving products rather than people—Fred Smith of Federal Express. Or the person who became a billionaire in the 1980s by discovering better ways of moving information between other people's computers—Ross Perot of EDS.

Prior to the past few decades, most of the greatest personal fortunes in American history—fortunes like those of the Astors (fur trading), the Rockefellers (oil), the Carnegies (steel), and the Fords (automobiles) were built on the bedrock of natural resources and manufacturing. Today, as evidenced by the financial difficulties of the richest families of just the past decade—the Hunts (oil and silver) or the Reichmans (real estate) the key to wealth no longer lies in owning or making physical assets but in distributing them.

CHAPTER V
Why Retailing in the 1990s
May Resemble Retailing in the 1950s

At the beginning of the 20th century, it was apparent that rapidly advancing technology would soon make the necessities of life affordable for every American family and that people would then stop working. By the 1930s many economists were predicting that, if government didn't institute higher and higher income tax rates, this rising affluence would lead to economic stagnation because people would become complacent when they obtained everything that they needed.

Today, we know that these economists were wrong because they failed to foresee that the same rapidly advancing technology would keep inventing new products which would keep expanding the average family's list of *necessities.*

"While technology keeps inventing new products and the average family's list of necessities continues to expand, only Network Marketing provides the most precious of all commodities: time freedom. Network Marketing gave me the money for a Lotus and airplane, but more importantly it gave me the time to enjoy them both."
                                                                    —Mark B. Yarnell

From Frederick Maytag's aluminum tub washing machine in 1922, to David Sarnoff's RCA black and white television set in 1939, the only thing growing faster than the affordability of existing products was the continual array of new products that kept adding to the American lifestyle. This spawned the unlimited consumer demand for goods and services which caused the United States to grow from an agrarian nation into the world's greatest economic power in less than a few decades.

One of the unsung heroes of this great economic boom was the department store, developed in the United States by such innovative retailers as Marshall Field's in Chicago (1865) and Filene's in Boston (1881). By using better technology to centralize the consumer credit, buying, and other functions of retailing, department stores quickly replaced the individual Main Street merchants from whom they themselves had sprung.

But these department stores did a lot more than just use technology to lower the cost of selling merchandise. The most important function they served was in educating their customers about the new products that would improve their lifestyles, fueling the never-ending cycle of consumer demand that defied then conventional economic logic. Instead of going to the department store to purchase something you wanted, you went to the department store to find out about something you didn't know existed but that you couldn't live without once you had learned about it.

Looking back on those days, before the advent of television and mass media, the department store alone served the two distinct functions of modern retailing—*education* and *distribution*. First, the department store *educated* its customers about new products that would greatly improve their lifestyles. Then, once it had taught the customer what was available and assisted them in choosing the right product for their needs, it *distributed* the product from the factory to the customer.

The traditional department stores fell into decline as advancing technology, like universal credit cards and shopping malls, made most of their original innovations obsolete. But perhaps nothing took as great a toll on them as the development of television and mass media—a development that allowed large manufacturers to bypass the traditional department stores entirely in communicating directly with their ultimate customers.

> *"When traditional department stores began their decline, new distribution companies like Amway began to dramatically prosper as they recognized that word-of-mouth advertising is by far superior to the media. As pointed out in the March 1992 edition of Success Magazine, many high-tech, Multi-Level Marketing companies are doing millions of dollars in monthly sales by emulating Amway instead of department stores, and all the while their independent distributors are becoming very wealthy."*
> **—Mark B. Yarnell**

Today most manufacturers "handshake" with their customers through the mass media, and the surviving retailers for most products are the lowest cost, most efficient, physical distributors of merchandise—like Wal-Mart, Target, and Toys R Us. These mass merchandisers almost exclusively distribute brand-name products to already educated consumers who know what they want. Customer loyalty has shifted from individual retailers—like Sears, Macy's and Safeway—to individual manufacturers or their products—like Sony, Levi's, and Proctor and Gamble.

Only twenty years ago, a commonly heard complaint about shopping in a retail store was that you, the customer, knew more than the clerks about what they were selling. Today, this isn't even newsworthy as most retail store shoppers assume that they are more educated about the products they want than the people who work there. Most surviving retailers have even abandoned the pretense of educating their sales clerks about the products they sell.

But with the abandonment by most retailers of their traditional educational function, we have lost for many items the ability to educate consumers about new products and services that will improve their lifestyles. A 30-second television commercial can do a great job convincing millions of already knowledgeable consumers to buy more Pepsi or Ivory Soap, but it is not going to educate consumers about some completely new product or service that they haven't heard about before.

> *"Network Marketing companies pay their distributors huge sums of override royalties which would have normally gone to the 'Madison Avenue' public relation firms of traditional retailers."*
> **—Mark B. Yarnell**

Certain products and services require one-on-one customer education that only a trained user of the product itself can provide. The list of these items include VCRs in the 1970s, telephone answering machines and services in the 1980s, and better vitamins and nutritional foods in the 1990s. Moreover, due to the lack of customer education vehicles today, there are many new products and services that, although they would greatly improve the lifestyles of their customers, have been around for several years but haven't yet made it to the mass marketplace.

For example, while interactive educational devices based on digital CDs would greatly improve the education of virtually every child in America, they have languished in libraries and research laboratories primarily because there has not yet emerged an efficient way to educate parents about them. Packaged foods manufacturers have had the ability for years to improve the healthfulness of their products with synthetic fats and oils, but have similarly not yet found a cost-efficient way to educate their customers about them.

One company that has retooled itself to serve the all-important educational function of traditional retailing is the Amway Corporation which started out in the 1960s as a distribution organization for proprietary soap products. Today's Amway distributors have virtually abandoned the physical distribution of their products and concentrate almost exclusively on educating themselves and their customers about new and innovative things that will improve their lifestyles. This has made Amway the retailer of choice for many of America's most innovative companies—particularly leading service organizations like MCI whose intangible products require one-on-one customer education.

> *"As companies like MCI have joined forces with Network Marketing firms in a successful effort to retail products and services, such alliances not only increased their profits, but have enhanced the image of the entire Network Marketing field. Today it is not uncommon for eminent corporate leaders and medical doctors to abandon their professions in order to capitalize on the wealth and time freedom afforded them through Network Marketing."*
> **—Mark B. Yarnell**

Another company that has very profitably capitalized on the need for customer education is Home Depot, Inc. which started in 1980 and quickly became the largest home improvement retailer in the nation. Home Depot prides itself most on having product specialists in virtually every category of home improvement—teaching customers not only what they need but even how to install it themselves.

In the future, technological developments like interactive television for ordering merchandise, and overnight or same-day shipping services for delivering it, may let many manufacturers bypass retailers entirely in physically distributing existing products to their ultimate consumers. This may one day eliminate the majority of retailers that concentrate on physical distribution, like Wal-Mart, in favor of retailers that concentrate on customer education, like Amway and Home Depot. This was evidenced right through the so-called Recession of 1991 when Amway's sales grew an incredible $0.8 billion from about $3.1 billion to $3.9 billion, or Home Depot's similar $1.3 billion rise in 1991 from $3.8 billion to $5.1 billion in annual sales.

However, the retailers specializing in customer education have a long way to grow before they seriously challenge the ones specializing in physical distribution. Traditional U.S. shopping center sales in 1991, mostly by the mass merchandisers like Wal-Mart and Sears, exceeded $717 billion.

"Network Marketing is no longer a little part-time business for the housewife who is merely seeking a few hundred dollars extra monthly income. As more and more high-powered entrepreneurs enter this field, traditional U.S. shopping centers will find themselves challenged by this new, highly lucrative form of distribution. Over the next decade, Network Marketing is projected to represent more than half the sales in America."
—Mark B. Yarnell

CHAPTER VI
What Your Son or Daughter Should Study in College

For most of us, life seems filled to capacity. There isn't even time to find out what we should learn to improve our lives.

And yet once we've found out about something that we know we should learn, we fight learning it. Even when we know that our lives could be easier, better, or more productive, we generally will devote more time trying to get around studying it than we eventually do learning it.

Of course once we do learn it, we become its greatest booster often turning to others exclaiming: "What, you haven't learned how to do that *yet*?"

This is one of the major problems with learning new things— a problem we sometimes perpetuate among our friends, our business associates, and even our family members without realizing it.

Most of us are afraid to learn new things. Even though we inherently know we can, we're scared—afraid that our boss or a loved one will find out that we're not really as smart as they think we are. This is particularly true of those of us who are very successful. Most highly successful people are motivated by their insecurities and the same insecurities that keep driving them for success also tell them that they "can't" when it comes to learning something new.

Then, once we have overcome this fear and learned something new, we often forget—perhaps subconsciously— how afraid we were when we first started out to learn it. And in forgetting how hard it was at first for us, we fail to express to others how scared we once were—implying that there's something wrong with them if they can't learn what we now know.

When I set out to teach someone something new, particularly to business associates or subordinates who may be intimidated about learning it, I ask them to first write down their fears and anxieties in a private journal. This way, afterwards, when they have to instruct the next person, they will be able to recall and pass on their anxieties—rather than perpetuate the myth that only the intellectually fearless can learn new things.

> *"What makes networking such a remarkable industry is that those who are most successful are those who can teach duplicable principles to the most people. Instead of jealously guarding success techniques, the real leaders in this industry pride themselves in sharing their formulas with everyone who will listen, making their success commensurate with the extent to which they help others."*
> **—Mark B. Yarnell**

One of the questions I am frequently asked by parents, particularly parents who have succeeded themselves but didn't have the opportunity to go to college, is what subject their son or daughter should study in college in order to achieve financial success.

I usually turn their question around, asking them detailed questions about what their son or daughter is really passionate about—sports, pets, movies, etc.—until they interrupt and tell me that they are asking my opinion about their child's economic welfare, not their child's social life. Then, I explain the answer to their original question.

The key to achieving financial success today, or success in any field for that matter, is being able to learn new things. And the key to having the ability to learn new things, is developing confidence in your ability to learn.

> *"Network Marketing develops self-confidence like no other field. The principles which yield success are very simple and easily duplicated by anyone with a sincere desire to learn. Among the most successful distributors in my organi-zation are brothers Dennis and David Clifton who were a student and police detective, re-spectively, prior to joining me in Network Mar-keting. Their skill was in their capacity to find leaders with the willingness to learn and the ability to teach others."*
> **—Mark B. Yarnell**

Even if there were one field or another that you could study in college for financial success, like "plastics" in the 1967 movie *The Graduate*, it wouldn't matter because most of what you studied in school would be technologically obsolete by the time you graduated. Today, it doesn't matter anymore how much you already know about a particular subject—things change so quickly that the most successful people in virtually every field are the people who learn new things the fastest.

Thus, the goal of every educational program should be to develop confidence in one's ability to learn. And the way to develop confidence about one's ability to learn is to learn some-thing very well. And the way to learn something very well is to be passionate about learning it.

The hope, then, for every parent concerned about their child's future economic welfare, is that the child discover an interest in anything—music, art, history, psychology, math — that they passionately want to learn about. If this happens, the child, on his or her own, will master learning about it and possibly even major in the subject eventually rising to the level where they will debate the subject with their professors.

If, and when, this happens, their future will be set—for they will have developed confidence in their ability to learn. This confidence in their ability to learn will lead them to success in whatever they seek.

Thus, if there is any gift a parent could give to a child, it is to nurture, whenever it occurs, the passion that a child might develop at any time to learn about any field or subject. For if the child masters learning just one subject, the parent who encouraged the child will have given a great gift. A true "gift of the magi," a gift that keeps on giving for the rest of their child's life.

"Children should be taught, above all else, that success results from finding work about which they are passionate and then pursuing that avenue. Eventually they will be paid more than they're worth because they are doing what they love. Network Marketing is such a field in that it builds self-confidence, leadership skills and communications excellence. Exposure to Network Marketing is indeed one of the greatest gifts any parents can give their children."
—Mark B. Yarnell

CHAPTER VII
Should You Quit Before You're Fired?

In 1931, a 21 year-old British college student won a traveling scholarship to the United States. The student was surprised to find that in a land of so much opportunity, most Americans wanted to work for large corporations, rather than strike out for themselves. He wrote a paper which attempted to answer the following question:

> Why, in a free enterprise economy, would a worker voluntarily submit to direction by a corporation instead of selling his own output or service directly to customers in the market?[1]

The student was Ronald H. Coase, the 1991 winner of the Nobel Prize for Economics.[2] The paper he wrote in 1931, which he later published as "The Nature of the Firm," explained why large corporations exist. And although the paper he wrote over 60 years ago is today one of the most frequently cited works in the field of economics, if Coase were to write this same paper today he might come to exactly the opposite conclusion.

Today, for exactly the same reasons that Coase cited in his landmark work (which we will examine in a moment), many large corporations should not exist. In fact, much of the unemployment we are experiencing today is actually the permanent dismantling of many of our large corporations— for reasons precisely described by Coase over half a century ago. Today, an employee of a large company might rightly ask whether they should quit the corporation now, before it inevitably quits them by going out of business.

In "The Nature of the Firm," Coase explained that the corporation exists because of its ability to reduce the *transaction costs* between individuals.[3]

For example, suppose a manager wants to dictate a letter and have it typed. The manager could hire someone just to type the letter, but the transaction costs of doing so—finding the typist, testing their skills, negotiating the price, etc.— would far exceed the cost of the work itself. To reduce these transaction costs, the manager trades away hiring only the exact amount of labor when and where he or she needs it. And the typist trades away his or her independence and higher compensation for a guaranteed time and place to work.

> *"The fundamental difference between those individuals who are still employed by corporations and those of us in Network Marketing is that, at some point, we refused to trade away our independence for a guaranteed income. In fact we realized that in traditional businesses there are no longer any guarantees at all!"*
> **—Mark B. Yarnell**

Coase also examined why businesses produced goods and services themselves that were available at less cost from outside firms—and he came to a similar conclusion. Businesses are often better off producing internally many of the things they need when one considers the transaction costs of dealing with outside suppliers.

Thus, according to Coase in the 1930s, large corporations exist as an efficient form of business organization because they reduce the transaction costs of doing business between different individuals and smaller firms.

However, as the large corporation continues to expand in size, different costs increase—the costs of managing workers, the costs of making erroneous decisions, and the costs associated with hiring personnel who are not directly compensated for their performance.

Coase wrote that the optimum size for the firm is that size at which these costs—the *inefficiency costs* inherent to being a large organization equal the *transaction costs*—the costs that the individuals would have to incur among themselves if they were free and independent agents.[4]

According to Coase, a corporation will continue to grow in number of employees as long as the reduced *transaction costs* of having more people working for the single entity exceed the increased *inefficiency costs* of having a larger organization.

Today, however, for exactly this reason, most large corporations should have far less employees. In fact, many large corporations should not even exist at all.

> *"Rational people are no longer willing to accept the fact that CEOs get 30% raises while massive layoffs are occurring and companies are losing money. As numerous corporations close their doors, and many others should over the next 20 years, the largest resource pool of unemployed professionals will emerge since the very inception of free enterprise. Network Marketing will fill that gap as one in three people will become prospects for our industry."*
> **—Mark B. Yarnell**

This is because over the past 60 years the transaction costs of doing business between different entities have dramatically fallen, while the inefficiency costs of a large corporation have dramatically risen.

The transaction costs of working with outside suppliers and workers communicating, delivering, accounting, etc.—are now so low relative to the value of the services or the materials being acquired that they are often no longer part of the decision-making process.

Moreover, these transaction costs—telephone calls, overnight services, computerized invoices—are expected to continue to decline.

Meanwhile, inefficiency costs have become a major component of doing business for large corporations. Since the inflationary 1960s, employees have gotten used to receiving an annual raise independent of their annual performance.

> *"In Network Marketing we create our own raises commensurate with the extent to which we apply ourselves. What scares people the most about our industry is the realization that perhaps for the first time in their life, they are going to find out what they are really worth. In reality you may be worth over $30,000 a month but have difficulty conceptualizing that fact."*
> **—Mark B. Yarnell**

It is now commonplace in many firms for two employees performing the exact same job—one newly hired and one with seven to ten years experience—to have a fifty percent or greater difference in their salaries.[5] Moreover, large organizations have become obligated to provide employees services such as health care and retirement benefits—costs that increase each year independent of the efficiency of their employees.

But the greatest reason that inefficiency costs have dramatically risen has been the relative ineffectiveness of the large corporation—compared to the individual entrepreneur—in implementing technological change.

Traditionally, the very term "large corporation" used to connote being on the cutting edge of technology. Computers were "mainframes" only used by large corporations, and only large corporations could afford to develop this technologically advanced equipment.

Today however, many of the largest firms in America— IBM, Xerox, Texas Instruments, Hewlett Packard, etc.—are themselves just providers of technology to third parties. The cutting edge of technology in most industries no longer belongs only to the large firm that can develop it themselves, but instead belongs to the entity or individual who can learn how to use the newest technology the fastest.

And the employees of large corporations, typically paid over the years more for their duration rather than their innovation, are sometimes the last to learn how to use the newest technology.

One way an employee can learn about where their particular employer may be heading is to look back on the raises that they have received. They should be able to clearly see how, directly from their increased efficiency or performance, the employer made at least as much more money as they received on each raise. If they cannot, it may be time to quit before they're fired because they may soon be terminated or a new competitor may soon put their company out of business.

> *"In Network Marketing no one can ever be terminated, thus, quitting becomes the only real block to one's eventual success. In addition, no competitive company ever put another Network Marketing company out of business. If there is genuine supply and demand, that simply can't happen in our industry."*
> **—Mark B. Yarnell**

1   Cheung. Steven N.S., "Ronald Harry Coase," *The New Palgrave: A Dictionary of Economics* (Macmillan Press Limited, London, 1987), 455.

2   Although Coase won the Nobel Prize for Economics in 1991, Coase is actually a Professor of Law who eschews mathematical analysis by so-called "economists."

3   While Coase's work in the 1930s is generally credited with founding the transaction cost approach to economic organization, he did not use the actual term "transaction cost" which only came into widespread use during the 1960s. Cheung, Steven N. S., "Ronald Harry Coase," 456.

4   Theoretically, a communist nation has the lowest transaction costs between individual workers and entities—since everyone works for the same "company," but the highest inefficiencies of waste and erroneous decisions—since individuals have the lowest individual incentives to work.

5   An employee receiving a seven to ten percent raise each year sees their salary double in as little as seven years.

Conclusions
by Rene Reid Yarnell

For years I have believed that 90% of the solution to any problem consists in the awareness of the problem. Most people live in denial whether they are plagued by alcoholism, stress or family difficulties. Denial, which is merely a self-imposed coping mechanism designed to protect the ego from information it can't handle, keeps many Americans tied to lives of mediocrity. Pick up any recent periodical from *Time* to *Psychology Today* and you'll likely encounter an article supporting Juliet Schorr's contentions in her latest book *The Overworked American* (Basic Books, 1991), that most of us are running ourselves into premature graves via the rat race. Everywhere we turn, noted specialists provide insights and daily revelations into the failure of traditional business to afford people the necessary time freedom to live balanced and meaningful lives.

What Mark and I have attempted to accomplish in this book of several of Professor Pilzer's latest essays is to illuminate the economic realities confronting each of us with the hope that your awareness will lead you out of denial. You should now ask yourself several pertinent questions and take the time to consider meaningful answers.

1. In spite of your title and income achievements, do you truly feel you are living life to the fullest?

2. Do you find yourself, as Professor Pilzer calls it, "trapped in the Red Queen's race—having to run faster and faster merely to stay in the same place?"

3. Do you agree that the old concept of going to school, finding the right company and working for that company for the rest of your life is, in Professor Pilzer's words, "a recipe for disaster?"

4. Should you quit before you're fired?

5. If your recipe for success has worked, is it duplicable and valuable to your children, friends and family members?

6. Do you realize that we are entering the Distribution Age and, unless you are poised and ready, you may miss your opportunity?

7. Do you realize that Network Marketing is the most viable method of distribution because of its minimal investment requirements and virtual lack of overhead?

8. Are you willing to admit that all the material things in the world shrink to insignificance compared with the most precious commodity of all—free time?

9. With the course you're on now, do you have a viable plan for your future?

10. Will you have the open-mindedness and wisdom, given these facts, to sit down for one hour with the person who introduced you to this book and take an honest and objective look at Network Marketing?

In traditional business, it is not *what* you know but *who* you know. In Network Marketing, it is not just *who* you know but who *they* know. On a scale of one to ten, you may rate yourself a five. But if you sponsor a ten, you become a ten.

When I became involved as an independent distributor for Nu Skin International, I was also a single parent, and held the responsible, elected position of county commissioner in Reno, Nevada. It really never occurred to me that I could earn *$100,000* a year part time, but that's exactly what occurred in my third year. Many professional people and leading corporate executives never earn that much working full time in their chosen fields. But what truly excites me as I look back on my career in networking is the freedom it has allowed both my husband and me. We spend a minimum of 20 hours a week in meaningful activities with our family. Last year we enjoyed several major vacations, and because our office is in our mountain retreat, we chose to reside in a forest setting in the beautiful Sierras just East of Lake Tahoe where each morning and evening we can commune with nature and enjoy the splendor of sunrises and sunsets.

When Senator Al Gore's close friend Patricia McCune needed the capital to found The International Green Cross, she called on us to help fund her first meeting with Mikhail Gorbachev at the Rio Summit. We had the money and time to help fund that project which now has a thousand new chapters in 75 countries. Imagine the satisfaction we feel to be co-founders of this organization, which could not have been possible had we not achieved the income and time freedom levels which only Network Marketing can afford us all.

But my purpose in these conclusive remarks is not to further acquaint you with our lives and the joy and serenity we've experienced so much as to help you achieve an awareness of precisely what new dimensions your life could take on, given the money and free time you deserve. With less stress and less focus on basic survival needs, you are more capable of devoting your energy toward making a real difference in your world. Professor Pilzer, as a noted and respected economist, has painted a graphic picture of current events without in any way suggesting that any solution, including Network Marketing, is a panacea for all our challenges.

Given the facts presented in these pages, and an understanding that Network Marketing has certainly been the solution for us, we simply wanted to provide you with a stimulating analysis. Hopefully, it will spur you onward in your desire to investigate non-traditional options.

We have, according to Charles Sykes, become "A Nation of Victims" (St. Martin's Press, 1992) with so many dependencies and disorders that those of us who aren't permanently disabled need to wear signs saying "temporarily abled." Most people live life aimlessly believing that, in the likely event they are unable to take care of themselves, there will always be a fallback—family, employer, government. In recent generations, we have been building a nation of people on mental welfare. The attitude of dependency is so deep-seated that recent insurance statistics report that by the time people reach the age of 65, 94% are living below poverty level. Social Security is providing a pittance of financial support to current recipients, but what will happen to Social Security with the aging of 76 million Baby Boomers? Few Baby Boomers (those born between 1946 and 1964) regard Social Security as any kind of security at all. They are willing to pay their dues now in return for extended quality of life in their later years with sufficient guaranteed residual income. Baby Busters (those born after 1965), having learned from their workaholic Boomer parents, want the financial security in their later years of life as well, but are more focused on having the time to enjoy it. It is the balance of the two, financial security and time freedom, that most of us are seeking in our lives.

To accomplish this we must take the first steps toward changing the attitude of mental welfare so deeply imbedded in our sub-consciousness. As a society, such dependency has stripped us of our dignity and self-worth. We are programmed to believe that performance will be rewarded if we put our faith in a company. And yet we all know how easily contracts with companies can be nullified. But if performance is tied to belief in ourselves and our own ability to succeed, that is where the breakdown occurs. To get people off the mental welfare doles and onto self-generating payrolls, they must be shown a way out. Network Marketing is the greatest opportunity in the history of free enterprise for creating self-sufficiency through residual income. But it will take people with vision and courage to see Network Marketing as a way out.

The blacksmiths who years ago laughed at the first automobiles to sputter down Main Street America, dismissing them as a passing fad, were soon out of work unless they had the open-mindedness to break through the narrow restrictions of their current paradigm, to investigate the newest field of transportation for ways in which they could participate. The reason the name Smith is most common in America is exemplary of the fact that at one time it was the most lucrative profession only to become obsolete within a mere three decades. There are still millions of Smiths left in America as every telephone directory will attest but few are shoeing horses and mending broken wagon wheels.

Network Marketing is currently "sputtering" down Main Street in every American city. You are welcome to join us in this newest of adventures in free enterprise. Remember, as Henry Ford once observed, "there are only two kinds of people in the world, people who think they can and people who think they can't ... and they're both right!" Given these facts, our hope is that you will begin to think you can, for truly therein, in that new positive self-image, lies the key to your destiny.

Rene Reid Yarnell
Reno, Nevada
November 1992

Foreword
By Mark B. Yarnell

When Terry Hill walked into my living room in the summer of 1986, it was about as unlikely a scenario as is conceivable. At the time I was an impoverished minister, recently converted to Network Marketing with no business or corporate experience, no college degree and no former entrepreneurial success. I had merely run an inexpensive ad in the sales section of the Austin newspaper soliciting people who were fed up with traditional business and desirous of achieving wealth and time freedom, both of which appealed to Terry.

She, on the other hand, was a well-educated young marketing professional who had recently been acknowledged as the #1 salesperson in Xerox. In fact, it was her third year to receive that honor. She laughingly now recalls that upon pulling into my driveway and discovering that our interview was being conducted in a small private home, she immediately decided to leave but was blocked from doing so as another vehicle pulled up behind her. She came inside ... and eventually resigned from Xerox in order to become involved totally in Network Marketing. Terry has since made millions of dollars and been the subject of numerous articles including a recent one in *Success Magazine*. More important to Terry is that she has a successful family life and plenty of time to enjoy her children and husband Tom, two things she was missing in corporate America. Tom also eventually resigned from Merrill Lynch as a very successful broker to join Terry in multi-level marketing shortly before they were married.

Although that meeting was interesting in many respects, it certainly was not atypical in the fascinating field of Network Marketing. Armed with little more than enthusiasm and tenacity, many housewives have recruited physicians away from their medical practices into this multi-level distribution industry. Unlikely people from extremely varied backgrounds often end up working together to build financial empires and subsequently become very close friends. Maids become partners with investment bankers and former attorneys general are recruited and trained by plumbers. Network Marketing is the great equalizer in that former successes are of little value and virtually anyone armed with a sincere desire to succeed and a hundred dollars to invest can launch a highly lucrative career in sales and recruiting.

What has been needed for quite some time is a brief book like this one written by a noted economist bold enough to honestly evaluate the factors which make networking such a viable industry. Paul Zane Pilzer is an outsider to this field, but a man who is quite capable of analyzing the economic factors which have created the perfect climate for the inevitable emergence of the distribution industry. Paul Zane Pilzer's great book *Unlimited Wealth* (Crown Publishers, 1991) drew immediate praise from both the media and his contemporaries for his fresh approach to economics.

When I was first granted the privilege to write the foreword and special commentary for this prelude to his newest work, I was both humbled and greatly appreciative that Professor Pilzer would trust me to tailor his analysis specifically to the Network Marketing industry. The mere opportunity to rub shoulders with a potential future Nobel Prize recipient is quite an honor, and I have done my very best to make certain that my ideas are absolutely consistent with his own. I frankly found the activity relatively easy because Professor Pilzer is essentially putting forth theories which we in Network Marketing have worked so diligently to promulgate for decades. We have been at odds with

To obtain further information on Professor
Paul Zane Pilzer, please contact:

ZCI Publishing
Dallas, Texas
(800) 460-4623
(214) 746-5555

To order additional copies of this book, or
for a current list of other materials by Mark
and Rene Reid Yarnell, please call:

(800) 458-TAPE